Presented to

_____

From

_____

_____

_____ *19* ___

International
CHILDREN'S
STORY
BIBLE

International
CHILDREN'S STORY BIBLE

————— Illustrated by —————
Children Around the World

WORD PUBLISHING
Dallas • London • Vancouver • Melbourne

International Children's Story Bible

Copyright 1990 by Word Publishing

Project coordinated by Laura Minchew
Stories edited by Mary Hollingsworth
Illustrations compiled by Lyn Rose

Library of Congress Cataloging-in-Publication Data

International children's story Bible/edited by Mary Hollingsworth.

    p. cm.

    Summary: A collection of 115 Bible stories from the Old and New Testament illustrated by children from around the world.

    ISBN 0–8499–0784–5 (Original Hardcover)

    ISBN 0–8499–1090–0 (Revised Hardcover)

    ISBN 0–8499–1097–8 (Handled)

    ISBN 0–8499–3533–4 (Softcover)

    ISBN 0–8499–3421–4 (Spanish)

    1. Bible stories. English. 2. Children's drawings. [1. Bible stories.
2. Children's art.] I. Hollingsworth, Mary, 1947–
BS551.2.I58   1990
220.9'505—dc20   90–44625
                                            CIP
                                            AC

Printed in the United States of America

6 7 8 9 LBM 14

Dear Parent:

Red and yellow, black and white, Jesus loves the little children . . . In this beloved refrain, we are assured of God's love for every person, regardless of race, nationality or culture. Yet, we often portray God's Word to our children through illustrations of people who look just like ourselves.

The ***International Children's Story Bible*** transcends racial, economic and cultural barriers and depicts favorite Bible stories through the eyes of children from around the globe. The young "artists" are from such places as Paraguay, Japan, France, Ireland, Kenya, Germany, Guatemala and most of the fifty United States. What an eye-opening experience to discover that a youth from Kenya pictures a black Abraham, an oriental child sees the three wise men as Japanese and the Roman soldiers drawn by children in Mexico are of hispanic descent.

As you read the Bible stories to your child, discuss with them how people in other countries view God and how much He loves each one of us. Something special happens when we see the Bible through the eyes of a child, especially the eyes of . . . *the little children of the world.*

May God greatly bless you and your child.

The Publisher

TABLE OF CONTENTS

Old Testament Stories

New Testament Stories

OLD TESTAMENT

STORIES

God Made Our World

In the beginning of time, God made the world and everything in it. Earth was empty and dark. So, the first thing God made was light. He made day and night. The second day God saw that water and land were all mixed up. So, He fixed that too.

God spent the next five days making the sun and moon, planting plants, making fish and birds. He made big animals and small animals. He made wild animals and tame animals. And He told each kind of animal to make more animals just like itself. Then God smiled because what He had done was very good.

But wait! God had one more thing He wanted to make.

GENESIS 1:1-25

Courtney Cooper, 7
Fort Worth, Texas, USA

Adam and Eve

On the sixth day, God made the most wonderful things of all. He made a man and a woman to be like Himself. And He named them Adam and Eve. God told Adam and Eve to take care of the earth. He put them in charge of everything—fish, birds, plants and animals. He showed them grain, fruit and green plants for them to eat. Then He told Adam and Eve to have lots of children.

Finally, God finished all His work. He saw that it was very good. So, on the seventh day, He rested.

GENESIS 1:26-2:3

Tiffany Babich, 11
Los Alamos, New Mexico, USA

Garden of Eden

Adam and Eve needed a place to live. So, God planted a beautiful garden for them called Eden. It was the most wonderful garden ever made. God planted all kinds of delicious fruit trees. In the middle of the garden He put the tree that gives life. That's also where God put the tree that gives knowledge of good and bad.

The garden of Eden was green and pretty. A river ran through the garden to water it and keep the plants growing. All the animals lived with Adam and Eve in Eden. Adam and Eve were very happy. But then they made a big mistake.

GENESIS 2:8-14

Ana Valadares, 13
Washington, DC, USA

Man's Big Mistake

God only had one rule in the garden. He told Adam and Eve, "Don't eat fruit from the tree that gives knowledge of good and bad. If you eat that fruit, you will die."

Now the snake talked to Eve. (The snake was really the devil.) "Eat the fruit," the snake said. "You won't die. Instead, you will be wise like God." Eve believed the snake. So, Eve ate the fruit. Then she gave some to Adam, and he ate it, too. That was a big mistake!

God punished Adam and Eve for disobeying Him. He made them leave the garden. He punished the snake, too. God made the snake crawl on his belly instead of walking. And he made women and snakes enemies forever.

GENESIS 2:15-17; 3:1-15

Shelley Croft, 10
Tigard, Oregon, USA

The First Brothers

Adam and Eve had two sons named Cain and Abel. Abel was a shepherd. Cain was a farmer. One day Cain brought God a gift of food he had grown. Then Abel brought God a gift of his best sheep. God liked Abel's gift but not Cain's. Cain felt angry and unhappy. He was so angry that he killed Abel.

God asked Cain, "Where is Abel?" Cain said, "I don't know. Is it my job to keep up with my brother?" God knew Cain had killed Abel. So, He punished Cain. God made Cain wander around the earth all his life. You see, brothers should love each other.

GENESIS 4:1-12

Amy Beckman, 10½
Boise, Idaho, USA

Noah's Boat

Noah was a good man who obeyed God. Everyone else had become bad. Being bad was all they thought about. One day God told Noah, "I am going to flood the earth. I will destroy every bad person and thing. But I will save you and your family. You must build a big boat." God told Noah exactly how to build the boat. So, Noah built the boat just as God said.

Then God sent two of each kind of animal and bird to Noah. Noah loaded all the animals and birds on the boat. Then he loaded his sons, their wives and Mrs. Noah. He did everything the Lord told him to do. Then drip-drip-drop; it started raining!

GENESIS 6:9-22

Hanan Jamalieh, 9
Nazareth, Israel

The Flood

After Noah loaded everyone on the big boat, God closed the door. Then came the flood. Water poured from everywhere! It came out of the springs underground. It fell from the clouds in the sky. The water got deeper and deeper. At last, the big boat floated.

Everything on earth was under water—even the mountains! It rained for 40 days and 40 nights. Everything and everyone on earth died. But Noah, his family and God's creatures on the boat were safe. They were safe and dry because Noah had done everything God told him to do. God protects those who obey Him.

GENESIS 7:11-24

Basil Khalil, 9
Nazareth, Israel

The Flood Ends

At last the rain stopped. When the water went down, the huge boat landed on the top of a mountain. Only the mountain tops were sticking up out of the water. About 40 days later Noah sent a dove out to find dry ground. But the dove could not find a place to land and came back. A week later Noah sent the dove out again. This time it brought back a small olive twig. Earth was almost dry! The next week when Noah sent out the dove, it didn't come back.

Then everyone got off the boat. God put a colorful rainbow in the sky. The rainbow showed God's promise never again to destroy the earth with water.

GENESIS 8:1-22

Dan Goodwin, 9
Upper Darby, Pennsylvania, USA

The Tower of Babel

At this time, everyone on earth spoke the same language. The people decided to build a city and a big, tall tower. They said, "We'll be famous! And we can all live in this city."

So, they began to build the city and tower. But God didn't want all the people to stay in one place. He made the people speak different languages. The people were confused when they couldn't understand each other anymore. The city became known as "Babel," which sounds like the word "confused" in the Hebrew language.

Since the people couldn't understand each other, they quit building the city. They moved to places all over the world. This was just what God wanted.

GENESIS 11:1-9

Craig Oertel, 11
Atlanta, Georgia, USA

Abram and Lot

One day God told Abram to move. God promised to take care of Abram and give him a big family if he would move. So, Abram, his wife Sarai and his nephew Lot took everything they owned and went to Canaan.

Both Abram and Lot were rich. They had so many animals that there was not enough grass to feed them. The men who cared for the animals began to fight over the land. Abram did not want their families to fight. So, he told Lot to choose which part of the land he wanted for his family. Abram and his family moved to the land Lot did not want. God does not want us to fight with our families.

GENESIS 12:1-13:13

Lilian Wangai, 8
Nairobi, Kenya

Esau Sells His Rights

Jacob and Esau were twins. But Esau was born first. So, when they grew up Esau would be given a bigger share of their father's wealth. Esau was a great hunter. Jacob worked near the family tents. One day Esau went hunting. He was gone so long that he came home weak from hunger. Jacob had made a pot of vegetable soup, and Esau asked for some.

Jacob said Esau could have some soup. But he would have to give Jacob his large share of their father's wealth. Esau was starving! So, he gave Jacob his share of the wealth. Then Jacob gave Esau some soup. Later, Esau was sorry he had sold his rights to wealth for just a bowl of soup. Sometimes we make mistakes when we're in a hurry.

GENESIS 25:20-34

Elsa Buckley, 9
Seattle, Washington, USA

Jacob's Dream

Jacob was traveling to Haran. When night came, he lay down to sleep. He used a rock as his pillow. While he was asleep, Jacob had a dream. In his dream he saw a ladder. The ladder reached from Earth all the way to heaven. Jacob dreamed he saw angels going up and down the ladder.

In his dream Jacob saw God standing at the top of the ladder. God said He would protect Jacob and give him a huge family. God also promised to give Jacob's family all the land where Jacob was resting. When Jacob woke up, he worshipped God.

GENESIS 28:10-22

Grant Gardner, 11
Konigstein, W. Germany

Joseph's Special Coat

Jacob had 12 sons, and Joseph was his favorite. Jacob gave Joseph a very special coat to show how much he loved him. But this made Joseph's older brothers jealous and angry.

One day Jacob sent Joseph to the field to check on his brothers. They were tending sheep. Joseph's brothers were still angry about his beautiful coat. So, they threw Joseph into an empty well. Then they dipped his special coat in goat's blood and took it to their father, Jacob. Jacob thought Joseph had been killed by a wild animal. He was very sad.

GENESIS 37:2-4, 18-24, 31-35

Abbie Ballou, 8
Springfield, Missouri, USA

Joseph Is Sold

While Joseph was in the well, his brothers saw some men coming on camels. The men were going to Egypt to trade and sell things. Joseph's brother, Judah, had an idea. He said, "Let's not kill Joseph. After all, he is our brother. Let's sell him to these men coming by."

Joseph's brothers sold him to the traders for eight ounces of silver. And the traders took Joseph with them to Egypt. But that's not the end of the story!

GENESIS 37:25-28

Emily Francis Jones, 9
Trinity, Alabama, USA

Joseph Explains The King's Dream

When Joseph was in Egypt, the king had a dream. He dreamed about seven full heads of grain and seven scrawny heads of grain. The scrawny heads of grain ate the seven full ones. Then the king woke up.

No one could explain the king's dream. But God helped Joseph understand what the king's dream meant. Joseph told the king, "There will be seven years of good crops. Then there will be seven years of bad crops and hunger. Choose someone wise to save food for the bad years." The king chose the wisest man he knew. He gave the job to Joseph.

GENESIS 41:22-40

Megan Culler, 10
Dublin, Ohio, USA

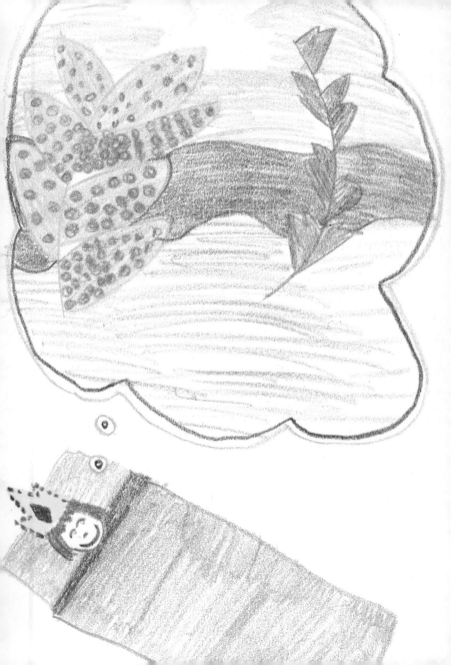

Joseph Rules Egypt

The king made Joseph ruler over all of Egypt. Only the King himself was more important than Joseph. During the seven years of good crops, Joseph built huge storehouses and saved the grain. Then during the famine, people from all over the world came to Egypt to get food.

Joseph's brothers came to Egypt to get grain. Joseph forgave his brothers for the mean things they had done to him. He brought his brothers and father to live with him in Egypt.

GENESIS 41:37-47:12

Joseph Griffith, 10
Columbus, Ohio, USA

Baby Moses

After Joseph died, an evil king ruled Egypt. He was afraid of Joseph's huge family, the Israelites. He thought they might take Egypt away from him. So, the bad king made a law that all Israelite baby boys should be drowned.

When Moses was born his mother hid him. She made a tiny boat out of grasses and tar. She put baby Moses in the little boat. And she put the boat in the Nile River.

The king's daughter came to the river. She found baby Moses crying. She felt sorry for Moses and adopted him. Moses grew up in the King's own house. And that's right where God wanted him.

EXODUS 1:8-2:10

Paul Edgerton, 9
Roseville, Minnesota, USA

A Burning Bush

After Moses grew up and left Egypt, he saw something very strange. Moses saw a bush that was on fire, but it didn't burn up! So, Moses went over to take a look. When Moses got near the burning bush, God spoke to him. God's voice was coming from the bush! He said, "Take off your shoes. You are on holy ground." Moses quickly took off his shoes. And he covered his face so he couldn't look at God.

God told Moses to go back to Egypt. He wanted Moses to help the Israelites escape. God wanted Moses to go ask the King of Egypt to let God's people leave. Moses went, but he was afraid.

EXODUS 3:1-4:23

Alexander Martinez, 8
Brooklyn, New York, USA

Ten Terrible Plagues

Moses and his brother Aaron went to see the king. They told him, "God says 'Let my people leave Egypt to worship me in the desert'." But the King said, "No." That made God unhappy.

God made terrible things happen in Egypt. He turned their water into blood. He covered Egypt with frogs, gnats and flies. The Egyptians' farm animals died. The people got sores on their bodies. A hail storm ruined the crops. Then locusts ate all the plants. It was completely dark for three days. God even caused the oldest child in each Egyptian's family to die. Finally, the King of Egypt let the Israelites go!

EXODUS 7:14-12:33

Samantha Bohannon, 10
Decatur, Alabama, USA

Leaving Egypt

God led the Israelites out of Egypt. His cloud led them during the day. His fire was with them at night.

The King of Egypt realized he'd lost all his slaves. He changed his mind about letting the Israelites leave. The king got his army together and chased the Israelites into the desert. He finally caught them at the shore of the Red Sea.

But God made a dry path for the Israelites through the sea. When the Egyptians followed them, the walls of sea water fell on the Egyptians. They all drowned. God had saved His people again!

EXODUS 14:5-31

Susan Turner, 8½
Winnipeg, Manitoba, Canada

God Sends Manna

The Israelites began to complain to Moses. They wanted meat to eat like they had eaten in Egypt. They mumbled and grumbled.

God heard them grumbling. He sent food down from heaven for them. In the evening quail covered their campground. In the early morning when the dew was gone, thin flakes lay on the ground. Moses told the Israelites that the flakes were sweet bread from heaven. The people called it "manna."

Each day the people gathered only enough quail and manna to eat that day. God sent more food every day. God took good care of His people.

EXODUS 16:1-21

Vera Marosi, 8
Nairobi, Kenya

Water From a Rock

The Israelites were traveling in the desert. Once, they camped at a place where there was no water. The people, their children and cattle were very thirsty. They complained to Moses, "Give us water to drink."

Moses asked God what to do. God told Moses to take his walking stick to Mount Sinai. On the mountain, God said for Moses to hit a rock with his walking stick. Water came out of the rock! The people drank all the cool water they wanted. Once again God helped His people.

EXODUS 17:1-7

Aron Mueller, 7
Anchorage, Alaska, USA

God's Ten Laws

God gave Moses ten laws to help keep the Israelites pure and holy. First, He told them not to worship any god but Him. Second, they were not to make any idols. Third, He told them not to misuse His name. Fourth, He said to keep the seventh day of the week holy. And fifth, He told them to honor their parents.

Sixth, God told the Israelites not to murder anyone. Seventh, they were not to break their marriage promises. Eighth, they were not to steal anything. Ninth, God said not to lie about their neighbors in court. And tenth, they were not to want to take their neighbor's things.

EXODUS 20:1-17

Travis Ashley, 9
Decatur, Alabama, USA

The Gold Calf

When God gave Moses the Ten Laws, he left the people and went up on a mountain. But Moses was gone so long, the people wondered if he was coming back. They begged Moses' brother, Aaron, to make an idol god. So, Aaron gathered the people's gold jewelry and melted it. Then he made an idol shaped like a calf. And the people began to worship it.

God saw what the people were doing and became angry. He sent Moses down the mountain to the people. Moses melted the gold calf. He crushed the gold into powder and poured it into the water. Moses made the people drink the water with gold in it.

God wants us to worship only Him.

EXODUS 32:1-20

Kacy Etheridge, 11
Oak Ridge, Tennessee, USA

The Twelve Spies

God told Moses to send 12 spies to explore Canaan. One leader from each of the 12 tribes of Israel went. The spies explored Canaan for 40 days.

When the spies returned, Joshua and Caleb said, "Let's go up and take the land. We can do it!" But the other ten spies were afraid. They said the people in Canaan were too big, and the cities were too strong. They even brought back a bunch of huge grapes. The Israelites listened to the ten spies. So, they didn't go and take Canaan as God had wanted.

God punished the Israelites. He made them stay in the desert for 40 more years. Only Joshua and Caleb got to go into Canaan.

NUMBERS 13:1-14:35

Jennifer Holland, 7
N. Little Rock, Arkansas, USA

A Talking Donkey

The Israelites were camped near Jericho, a city in Moab. The king of Moab was afraid of them. He sent for Balaam to come and put a curse on the Israelites.

God did not want Balaam to go. Three times, God sent an angel to block Balaam's path. Each time Balaam's donkey saw the angel and stopped. But Balaam did not see the angel. So, Balaam got very mad and hit the donkey to make him go. Finally, God made the donkey talk to Balaam. The donkey said, "Why are you hitting me?"

Then God showed Balaam the angel. Balaam realized the donkey was trying to protect him. He was very sorry and decided to do what God wanted.

NUMBERS 22:1-34

Micah Beard, 9
Bangor, N. Ireland

Rahab Helps the Spies

Joshua sent two men to spy on Jericho. They stayed at Rahab's house. The bad king found out the spies were in Jericho. He sent soldiers to find them. Rahab hid the spies on her roof under some plants. She told the soldiers the spies had already left. Rahab helped the spies escape. She let them down from her window over the wall of the city with a red rope.

The spies told Rahab to hang the red rope in her window, and they would protect her. When Israel attacked Jericho, the spies saved Rahab and her whole family.

JOSHUA 2:1-24; 6:22-25

David Richardson, 12
Washington, England

The Sun Stands Still

Five kings of Amon put their armies together and attacked Gibeon. The people in Gibeon sent a message to Joshua to come and help them. Joshua's army marched all night to Gibeon. And they surprised the kings of Amon. Joshua's army chased the Amonites away.

That day the Lord let the Israelites defeat their enemies. Joshua prayed for the sun to keep shining so they could keep winning. God made the sun and moon stand still for a whole day! That had never happened before that day. And it has never happened since.

JOSHUA 10:5-14

Ashley Miner, 6
Terre Haute, Indiana, USA

Gideon's Brave 300

Gideon's army was getting ready to fight their enemies, the Midianites. The Midianites had a huge army. Gideon had 32,000 men, but God told Gideon, "You have too many men. Send all those home who are afraid." So, 22,000 men went home. God helped Gideon narrow his army down to 300 men. Finally, Gideon's 300 brave men were left to fight the huge Midianite army.

Gideon's army went at night and surrounded their enemies. Gideon's army took only jars, trumpets and torches for weapons. They blew the trumpets and broke the jars. And the Midianites ran away!

JUDGES 7:1-22

Raymond Kotzatoski, 8
Altoona, Pennsylvania, USA

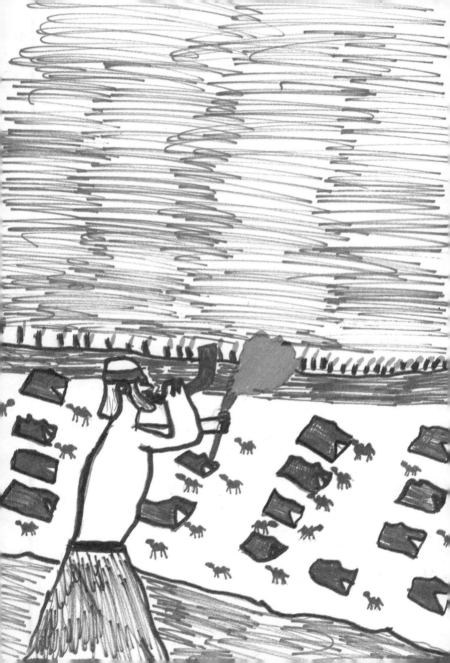

Samson and Delilah

Samson was the strongest man God ever made. The secret of his strength was his long hair. As long as his hair was not cut, Samson would be strong.

Samson loved a bad woman named Delilah. Samson's enemies told Delilah, "Find out what makes Samson strong. Help us capture him. And we will pay you lots of money."

Delilah tricked Samson into telling her the secret that his long hair made him strong. Delilah told Samson's enemies his secret. Then, while Samson slept, a man cut off his hair. When Samson woke up, he was weak. His enemies captured him. Samson should not have told anyone his secret.

JUDGES 16:4-22

Penny Broadhurst, 9
Hampsthwaite, England

The Story of Ruth

Naomi's son married Ruth. After several years both Naomi's husband and Ruth's husband died. So, Naomi decided to move back to her homeland. But Ruth would not leave Naomi. She went with Naomi.

Ruth worked hard to take care of Naomi. She picked up grain in a field that belonged to Boaz. He was Naomi's relative. Boaz wanted to marry Ruth. But he had one problem. Naomi had a closer relative than Boaz. The relative had first choice to take care of Ruth. Boaz talked to the other relative. But the relative could not take care of Ruth. So, he let Boaz marry Ruth. Boaz and Ruth had a baby named Obed. And Naomi took care of the baby. They were all very happy.

RUTH 1-4

Minda Johnson, 8
St. Paul, Minnesota, USA

David and Goliath

Goliath was a nine-foot-tall soldier from Gath. He bragged that he could beat any Israelite soldier who would fight him. But all the Israelite soldiers were afraid to fight him.

David was a young shepherd boy who believed in God. He said, "I'll fight Goliath. The Lord will help me beat him." David took five smooth stones from the brook and his sling. Then, he went to fight Goliath. Goliath laughed at the boy coming out to fight him. But David threw a stone with his sling at Goliath. It hit Goliath in the forehead and knocked him down. Then David took Goliath's sword and killed him. David believed in God, and God helped David beat the giant.

1 SAMUEL 17:32-51

Jamie Harrison, 12
Omaha, Nebraska, USA

David and Jonathan

Jonathan and David were very good friends. David heard that Jonathan's father, King Saul, wanted to kill him. Jonathan loved David. So, when Jonathan found out that King Saul did want to kill David, he went to warn him.

Jonathan took his arrows and a servant boy to chase the arrows. They went out to the field where David was hiding. Jonathan shot an arrow past the servant boy as a signal to David.

Then David and Jonathan cried and said goodbye. David's friend had saved his life. And they stayed friends for the rest of their lives.

1 SAMUEL 20:1-42

David Shaffer, 12
Cotuit, Massachusetts, USA

King Solomon's Wisdom

Solomon was King David's son. He became king of Israel when David died. One day God said to Solomon, "Ask for anything you want. I will give it to you." Solomon asked for wisdom to lead God's people. God was very happy. He made Solomon the wisest man to ever live.

One day two women brought a baby to Solomon. Each woman said the baby was her child. Solomon said, "Cut the baby in half and give half of the baby to each woman." "NO!" screamed the real mother, "Give my baby to her." Then Solomon knew who the real mother was because of the way she loved the baby. He gave the baby to its real mother.

1 KINGS 3:5-28

Katie A. Perkins, 8
Ft. Worth, Texas, USA

Elijah Stops the Rain

Ahab was a bad king of Israel. He did many wrong things. Elijah was one of God's prophets. One day Elijah went to see King Ahab. He told the king, "I serve the Lord, the God of Israel. I am telling you the truth. No rain or dew will fall during the next few years unless I command it."

God knew that Ahab would be mad at Elijah. So, God hid Elijah near the Jordan River. He sent ravens with food to feed Elijah every day. Just as Elijah said, it didn't rain in Israel for three years!

1 KINGS 16:29-30; 17:1-6

Kelly Taylor, 8
Springfield, Missouri, USA

Elijah and the Prophets of Baal

Three years passed with no rain. Finally, God told Elijah, "Go and meet King Ahab. I will soon send rain." So, Elijah told Ahab to bring the 450 prophets of the false god Baal to Mount Carmel for a contest. The prophets of Baal built an altar and put a dead bull on it. They called on Baal to set the bull on fire. But nothing happened.

Then Elijah built an altar and put a dead bull on it. He poured 12 huge jars of water on his sacrifice. Then he asked God to set it on fire. God sent fire from heaven to burn up the bull, the altar and even the stones. Then all the people worshipped God.

1 KINGS 18:1-39

Kristin Mueller, 11
Anchorage, Alaska, USA

A Boy Lives Again

One day a little boy died. His mother ran to get Elisha to help her. Elisha went into the room with the child and closed the door. Elisha prayed to God. He placed his body on top of the boy's body. He put his eyes on the boy's eyes. His hands were on the boy's hands. He put his mouth on the boy's mouth. Then a miracle happened! The boy's skin began to get warm.

Elisha walked around the room. He covered the boy again. This time, the boy sneezed seven times and opened his eyes. He was alive!

2 KINGS 4:18-37

Patrick Williams, 8
Shreveport, Louisiana, USA

Queen Esther Saves Her People

Haman was the most important man in King Xerxes' kingdom. But he hated the Jewish people. He tricked King Xerxes into making a bad law to kill all the Jews. Now, Esther was the Queen, and she was a Jew. So, Esther decided to tell the king of Haman's trick. But the Queen was not supposed to go see the king unless he sent for her. If she did, the king could have her killed.

Brave Esther dressed in her best clothes and went to the king. The king loved Esther and he let her come in. Then she told him about Haman's evil plan. King Xerxes became very angry. He had Haman hanged. Queen Esther had saved her people.

ESTHER 2-7:10

Josse Rocio Santizo Gil, 10
Guatemala, Guatemala

Job Is Faithful

Job was a great man. He was honest and good. He honored God and not evil. He had lots of children, animals and helpers.

Satan (the devil) caused Job to lose everything he had—children, animals, helpers—everything! Satan caused Job to have terrible sores on his body. Job's friends said he must have been very bad and made God angry. But that wasn't true. Even Job's wife told him to curse God and die. But Job loved God and worshipped Him through all his troubles.

At last, God gave Job everything he had before . . . and a lot more! Job was faithful to God, so God rewarded him. God always rewards those who love Him.

JOB 1-41

Cory Sheldon, 12
Stow, Ohio, USA

My Shepherd

The Lord is like a shepherd to me. A shepherd takes care of his sheep. The Lord takes care of me. He gives me everything I need. He gives me nice places to rest and good water to drink. He helps me to be strong.

He helps me do the right things. Even when something sad happens, I am not afraid. I know the Lord will be with me.

The Lord makes me strong when I face my enemies. He honors me. He gives me more than I need. I know God will love me all my life. And I will live with Him forever.

PSALM 23

Sarah Ratliff, 7
Alamogordo, New Mexico, USA

Advice to Children

My child, remember these teachings. Remember these rules. Then you will live a long time. And your life will be good.

Don't ever stop being kind. Always tell the truth. Be kind to everyone, and people will respect you. You will please God and other people, too.

Trust the Lord with all your heart. Don't depend on yourself, but depend on the Lord. Then He will give you success.

Respect the Lord, and refuse to do wrong. Then you will have a healthy body and strong bones. If you do these things, you will be happy.

PROVERBS 3:1-8

Jennifer Yactor, 11
Los Alamos, New Mexico, USA

The Blazing Furnace

A certain king had the people make a huge gold idol. It was 90 feet tall and 9 feet wide. The king told the people, "When you hear the music play, everyone must bow down to the idol. If you don't bow down, you will be thrown into a blazing furnace."

Now, Shadrack, Meshack and Abednego believed in God. And they wouldn't bow down to the idol. So, the king had them thrown into the fiery furnace. But when he looked into the fire, the king saw four men—not three. None of them were burned in the fire! The king was amazed. God had saved Shadrack, Meshack and Abednego. Then the king told all his people to honor God.

DANIEL 3:1-30

Jeremy Young, 11
Oklahoma City, Oklahoma, USA

Writing on the Wall

King Belshazzar was having a big banquet. Suddenly, a person's hand appeared and wrote on the wall. King Belshazzar was afraid. His face turned white. And his knees shook. He was too weak to stand up.

The king's wise men could not read the words. So, Daniel, who loved God, told the king what the words meant. Daniel said, "Your kingdom is about to end. God has weighed you on His scales, and you're not good enough. Your kingdom is being divided."

The king promoted Daniel to a very high position in his kingdom. But that very night the king was killed. God's words are true.

DANIEL 5:1-31

Steven Thomas, 11
Ft. Worth, Texas, USA

Daniel in the Lions' Den

Daniel was the best man in King Darius' kingdom. He loved God and prayed to Him three times each day. Some bad men were jealous of Daniel. They tried to get him in trouble.

The men tricked King Darius into making a law. The law said no one could pray to anyone but Darius for 30 days. Anyone who prayed to God would be thrown into the lions' den. But Daniel still prayed to God. The bad men told the king. So, the king put Daniel in the lions' den.

God protected Daniel. The next morning the king found Daniel alive. God had closed the mouths of the lions! Then the happy king and all his people believed in God.

DANIEL 6:1-28

Yuriko Emaru, 8
Iruma Shi, Japan

Jonah and the Big Fish

God told Jonah to go preach in Nineveh. But Jonah didn't want to go. So, he ran away from God. He got on a ship going away from the place God told him to go. God caused a big storm on the sea. The ship was about to sink! The men on the boat discovered that the storm was Jonah's fault. So, they threw Jonah into the sea.

Now, God sent a big fish to swallow Jonah. Jonah stayed in the belly of the fish for three days. Finally, God made the fish spit Jonah out on the dry ground. At last Jonah listened to God and went to Nineveh. It's always best to do what God says.

JONAH 1:1-3:10

Sarah Carr, 7
Asuncion, Paraguay

NEW TESTAMENT

STORIES

An Angel Visits Mary

Mary was a virgin who lived in Nazareth. She was engaged to marry Joseph. God sent His angel Gabriel to visit Mary. The angel told Mary that God was very pleased with her. He said Mary was going to have a baby. The baby would be the Son of God! And she should name the baby Jesus.

Mary said, "I am God's servant. Let this happen as you say." Then the angel went away. And that's the beginning of the most wonderful story of all.

LUKE 1:26-38

Sarah Gentry, 11
Somerset, New Jersey, USA

Jesus Is Born

It was almost time for Mary's baby to be born. Mary and Joseph had to travel from Nazareth to Bethlehem. They had to be counted in a census.

In Bethlehem, the time came for Mary to have the baby. Mary and Joseph tried to find a nice room in one of the inns. But all the rooms were taken. So, Mary and Joseph had to stay in a stable. Mary gave birth to baby Jesus in a stable! Mary wrapped baby Jesus with cloths and used the animals' feeding box for his bed. It was a happy time for the whole world!

LUKE 2:1-7

Ryan Gates, 11
Cuyahoga Falls, Ohio, USA

Shepherds Hear About Jesus

The night Jesus was born, some shepherds were watching their sheep in a field near Bethlehem. Suddenly, they saw God's angel. The shepherds were afraid. The angel said, "Don't be afraid. I am bringing you good news. All the people will be happy. Today your Savior was born in Bethlehem! He is Christ the Lord."

Then the shepherds hurried to Bethlehem to see baby Jesus. They found Mary and Joseph in the stable. And they found the baby in the feeding box. Then the shepherds praised God for Jesus!

LUKE 2:8-20

Lisa Paden, 11
Libby, Montana, USA

Wise Men Come to Jesus

When Jesus was born some wise men saw His special star. So, they followed the star a long way to see the Savior. The wise men asked, "Where is the baby who was born to be the king of the Jews? We have come to worship Him."

King Herod was upset about baby Jesus, because he thought Jesus would be king instead of him. So, Herod tried to trick the wise men. He asked the wise men to find Jesus and tell him where Jesus was. Herod lied and said he wanted to worship Jesus, too.

When the wise men found Jesus, they gave Him special gifts of gold and perfume. And they worshipped Him.

MATTHEW 2:1-12

Tomoko Yamaguchi, 8
Tokorozawa, Japan

Escape to Egypt

The wise men did not tell King Herod where Jesus was staying. God had warned them about Herod's trick. Then God's angel spoke to Joseph in a dream. The angel said Herod was going to try and kill Jesus. So, Joseph, Mary and Jesus escaped to Egypt in the middle of the night.

Herod gave an order to kill all the baby boys in Bethlehem and around the city. He said to kill every baby boy who was less than two years old. But they did not find Jesus.

Joseph, Mary and Jesus stayed in Egypt until Herod died. Then they went home to Israel.

MATTHEW 2:13-20

Laura Clark, 9
Woodville, Ohio, USA

The Boy Jesus

When Jesus was 12, He went with His parents to Jerusalem. A few days later, Mary and Joseph started home. They thought Jesus was with their family and friends in the group. They traveled a whole day. But Mary and Joseph could not find Jesus. They went back to Jerusalem to look for Him.

Mary and Joseph looked for Jesus three whole days! Then they found Him in the Temple. He was with the religious teachers. Mary said, "Son, why did you do this? We have been very worried." But Jesus said, "You should have known I must be where my Father's work is." Then Jesus went home with His parents. And He did everything they told Him to do.

LUKE 2:41-51

Jon-Marc Harrison, 10
Omaha, Nebraska, USA

John the Baptist

John was a preacher who lived in the desert. John's clothes were made from camel's hair. For food, he ate locusts and wild honey. Many people went to hear John preach. He taught the people to be baptized. He taught them to change their hearts and lives so their sins could be forgiven.

Some people thought John might be Christ the Savior. But John told them, "I baptize you with water. But Someone is coming later who can do more than I can. He will baptize you with the Holy Spirit and with fire." John was telling them about Jesus!

MATTHEW 3:1-12

Andrew Beckwith, 7
Higashi Kurume, Japan

Jesus Is Baptized

Jesus came to have John baptize Him. But John tried to stop Jesus. John said, "Why do you want me to baptize you? You should be baptizing me!"

Jesus said, "Let it be this way for now, John. We must do all things that are right." So John baptized Jesus. When Jesus came up out of the water, heaven opened. God's Spirit came down on Jesus like a dove. Then a voice spoke from heaven. The voice said, "This is my Son and I love Him. I am very pleased with Him."

MATTHEW 3:13-17

Valerie Valenzuela, 9
Nairobi, Kenya

Jesus Is Tempted

God's Spirit led Jesus into the desert to be tempted by the devil. Jesus did not eat for 40 days and nights. He was very hungry. The devil said, "If you are God's Son, turn these rocks into bread." But Jesus told the devil this Scripture: "A person does not live only by eating bread."

Then the devil told Jesus, "Jump off the top of the Temple. The angels will protect you. But Jesus said, "Do not test the Lord your God." Finally, the devil promised Jesus the whole world if Jesus would worship him. But Jesus said, "Get away from me, Satan! We must worship only God." Then the devil left Jesus alone. We must stand up to the devil as Jesus did.

MATTHEW 4:1-10

Meggie Anderton, 8
Knoxville, Tennessee, USA

The Lord's Prayer

Jesus taught His followers to pray
like this:
"Our Father in heaven,
we pray that Your name will always
be honored. We pray that your
kingdom will come.
We pray that what you want
will be done,
here on earth as it is in heaven.
Give us the food we need for each day.
Forgive us for doing wrong things,
and help us forgive others.
Do not cause us to be tested. But save
us from Satan's tricks."

MATTHEW 6:9-13

Kareen Hansen, 9
Nairobi, Kenya

Jesus' Sermon on the Mountain

Crowds of people followed Jesus everywhere. They wanted to hear Him teach. One day Jesus saw the crowds who had gathered. Jesus went up on the side of a mountain so the people could hear Him. He taught the people many important things.

He taught them how to be happy. He taught them about loving and giving. He taught them about prayer and worship. And He taught them to treat other people as they wanted to be treated. When Jesus finished teaching, the people were amazed!

MATTHEW 5-7

Saida Helaine Cedeno Freites, 10
San Antonio de los Altos, Venezuela

Jesus Feeds More Than 5,000 People

A large crowd followed Jesus to a faraway place. Late that afternoon, Jesus' followers came to Him. They told Him there was no place nearby to get food. They thought Jesus should send the people away so they could go get something to eat. But Jesus told His followers to feed all the people themselves.

Jesus' followers said, "But we only have five small loaves of bread and two fish." So, Jesus told them to bring the bread and fish to Him. Jesus thanked God for the food and divided the bread. His followers gave the food to the people. More than 5000 people were fed. Everyone ate until he was full. And 12 baskets of food were left!

MATTHEW 14:13-21

Merry Adis Prasetya Polly, 11
Kupang, NTT, Indonesia

Jesus Walks on Water

Jesus' followers were crossing the lake in a boat. The wind and waves were very strong and were tossing the boat around. Jesus saw that His followers were in trouble. He started walking toward the boat on top of the water. When His followers saw Him walking on water, they were afraid. They thought He was a ghost! But Jesus said, "It is I. Don't be afraid."

Peter said, "Lord, if it's you, let me walk to you on the water." Jesus said, "Come." Then Peter walked on water like Jesus! But Peter saw the wind and waves and was afraid. He began to sink and shouted, "Lord, save me!" So, Jesus reached out and saved him. Jesus can save you, too.

MATTHEW 14:22-31

Shannon Payne, 9
Taos, New Mexico, USA

Jesus Enters Jerusalem

Jesus' followers borrowed a donkey and her colt for Jesus to ride into Jerusalem. Then they laid their coats on the donkeys, and Jesus rode them into the city.

Many people spread their coats on the road before Jesus. Others cut branches from the palm trees and spread them on the road. Some of the people were walking ahead of Jesus. Others were walking behind Him. All the people were shouting, "Praise to the Son of David! God bless the One who comes in the name of the Lord! Praise to God in heaven!" Jesus rode into Jerusalem as a King. And the people of the city were very excited.

MATTHEW 21:1-11

Pamela E. Villegas, 10
Pasig, Metro Manila, Philippines

Jesus Cleans Out the Temple

Jesus went to the Temple. He saw that the people who were buying and selling things there were cheating each other. This made Jesus very angry!

Jesus turned over the tables of the men who were exchanging money. And He knocked over the benches of the people who sold doves in the Temple. Jesus told the people, "The Scriptures say, 'My Temple will be a house where people will pray.' But you are turning God's house into a hideout for robbers."

MATTHEW 21:12-13

Christen Williams, 11
Burleson, Texas, USA

A Paralyzed Man Is Healed

Jesus was teaching in a very crowded house in Capernaum. The house was so full that no one else could come in. Four people carried their paralyzed friend to see Jesus. But they couldn't get into the house. So, they made a hole in the roof of the house. Then they lowered their friend down to Jesus. Jesus saw their great faith. He said, "Your sins are forgiven."

Some teachers of the law were shocked. They didn't think Jesus could forgive sins like God. Jesus knew what they were thinking. To prove He was God, Jesus healed the paralyzed man. The man got up and walked. Everyone was amazed!

MARK 2:1-12

Jennifer Sims, 9
Lakewood, Colorado, USA

Jesus Stops a Storm

Once Jesus asked His followers to go across the lake with Him. They all got in a boat. A very strong wind came up. Waves crashed into the boat. The followers were scared. But Jesus was sleeping through the storm. The followers woke Jesus up. They said, "Don't you care about us? We will drown in this storm!"

Then Jesus stood up. He told the wind and waves to stop. He said, "Quiet! Be still!" Then the wind stopped. And the lake became calm. The followers asked each other, "What kind of man is this? Even the winds and waves obey Him." Jesus is more powerful than nature.

MARK 4:35-41

Jennifer Hodgson, 11
Springfield, Missouri, USA

Jesus Loves Children

Some people were bringing their small children to Jesus. They wanted Jesus to touch the children. But His followers told the people to go away. When Jesus saw this, it made Him unhappy. He said to His followers, "Let the children come to me. Don't stop them. God's kingdom belongs to people who are like these little children."

Then He said, "You must accept God's kingdom as a child accepts things. If you don't, you will never get in." Then Jesus took the children in His arms. He put His hands on them and blessed them. Jesus loves children.

MARK 10:13-16

Shauna McNalley, 11
Toronto, Ontario, Canada

Jesus Heals a Blind Man

When Jesus and His followers were leaving Jericho they passed a blind beggar. The blind man shouted, "Jesus, Son of David, please help me!"

Many people told the blind man to be quiet. But he kept shouting to Jesus. Finally, Jesus told the people to bring the man to Him. Jesus said, "What do you want me to do for you?" The blind man said, "I want to see again, Teacher." Then Jesus healed him. Jesus loves handicapped people, too.

MARK 10:46-52

Alisha Echols, 11
Leslie, Arkansas, USA

A Poor Woman's Great Gift

One day Jesus was sitting near the money box in the Temple. This box is where people put their money gifts to God. Some rich people gave lots of money. One very poor woman came and gave two small coins. These coins were worth less than one penny.

Jesus said to His followers, "This woman just gave two coins. But she really gave more than all those rich people. The rich gave only what they did not need. This woman is very poor. She gave all the money she had." God loves true givers.

MARK 12:41-44

Rebekah Carter, 11
Buenos Aires, Argentina

A Woman Shows Kindness

Jesus was at Simon's house for dinner. A woman came and poured expensive perfume on Jesus' head. Some people became angry. They said, "Why waste that perfume? It was worth a full year's pay. She should have sold the perfume and given the money to the poor."

Jesus said to them, "Don't bother the woman. She has done a beautiful thing for me. You can always help the poor. But I won't be here for long. She has done the only thing she could for me before I die. The story of her kindness will always be told so people will remember her."

And, sure enough, here we are telling her story again!

MARK 14:3-9

Molly Corkle, 10
Lincoln, Nebraska, USA

Fishers of Men

Jesus had been sitting in Peter's boat teaching people on the shore. Then He told Peter to take his boat into deep water and he would catch some fish. Peter said, "Master, we've fished hard all night and caught nothing. But we'll try again, if you say so."

The fishermen put their nets in the water. They caught so many fish their nets started to break! Their two boats were so full of fish that they began to sink. The fishermen were amazed! Jesus said, "From now on you will fish for men." Jesus meant they would tell people about Him. We should be fishers of men, too.

LUKE 5:1-11

Jonathan Reinhardt, 9
Berlin, W. Germany

The Good Samaritan

Jesus told this story: "Some bad men attacked a Jewish man. They beat him and robbed him. They tore off his clothes and left him to die. Two religious men came by. They saw the hurt man, but they did not stop to help.

"Then a Samaritan man came by. Now, Jews and Samaritans were enemies. But when the Samaritan saw the hurt Jewish man, he stopped to help. He doctored the man's wounds. He put the hurt man on his own donkey and took him to an inn. He took care of the Jewish man. Then he gave the innkeeper some money to continue caring for the man."

We should be good neighbors, too, just as the Samaritan was to the Jewish man.

LUKE 10:30-37

Lydia Harlan, 8
San Marcos, California, USA

The Lost Sheep

Many sinners came to hear Jesus preach. The religious leaders complained, "Look! Jesus welcomes sinners and even eats with them."

So, Jesus told this story: "Suppose a man had 100 sheep, but one got lost. He would leave the 99 sheep alone and go look for the lost one. He would keep searching until he found the sheep. And when he found it, he would be very happy. He would say to his friends and neighbors, 'Be happy with me. I have found my lost sheep!' In the same way, there is much joy in heaven when one sinner changes his heart. The other 99 don't need to change."

LUKE 15:1-7

Curtis Crutcher, 8
West Jordan, Utah, USA

The Wasteful Son

Jesus also told this story: "A father had two sons. The younger son took his share of his father's money and left home. He went to a country far away. There he wasted all his money. There was no rain in that country. And there was no food. The son needed money. So, he got a job feeding pigs. He was so hungry he was willing to eat the pigs' food. The son was sorry he had done wrong. He decided to go home and ask his father to forgive him.

"When he was almost home, his father saw him coming. The father ran out and hugged and kissed him. Then he gave a party to welcome his son back home." God loves you just as this father loved his son.

LUKE 15:11-24

Michael Frazee, 9
Knoxville, Tennessee, USA

Jesus Heals Ten Men

Jesus met ten men who had a bad skin disease. They called out, "Jesus! Master! Please help us!" Jesus told the men to go and show themselves to the priests. While the men were on their way to the priests, Jesus healed them. But only one man went back to thank Jesus.

Jesus said, "Ten men were healed. Where are the other nine? Are you the only one who came back to say 'thank you'? Stand up and go on your way. You were healed because you believed." We should thank God for His blessings.

LUKE 17:11-19

Amanda McNalley, 11
Toronto, Ontario, Canada

Zaccaheus Meets Jesus

Jesus was traveling through Jericho. Zacchaeus wanted to see Jesus. But he was too short to see over the crowd. So, Zacchaeus climbed up in a tree. When Jesus came to the tree, he saw Zacchaeus. He said, "Zacchaeus come down. I must stay at your house today."

Zacchaeus was happy to have Jesus in his house. Other people complained that Jesus should not have stayed with Zacchaeus, because Zacchaeus was a tax collector who stole money. But Zacchaeus repented of his evil ways. Jesus saved him! That's why Jesus came to earth—to save sinners.

LUKE 19:1-10

Michelle Miller, 12
Atlanta, Georgia, USA

Jesus Heals an Officer's Son

An important soldier lived in the city of Capernaum. The soldier's son was so sick he was about to die. So, the soldier went to Jesus and begged Him to come and heal his son.

Jesus said, "Go home. Your son will live." The man believed Jesus and started home. On the way, the man's servants came to meet him. They told him his son was well. The soldier asked his servants what time the son had gotten well. They said it was about one o'clock. The man knew that was the exact time Jesus had said his son would live! Then the man and his family trusted Jesus. Jesus can make sick people well.

JOHN 4:46-53

Carlos Stuardo Santizo Paz, 11
Guatemala, Guatemala

A Sick Man at Siloam

In Jerusalem there was a pool with five covered porches. Many sick people were lying on the porches beside the pool. Some were blind, some were crippled and some were paralyzed. One man had been sick for 38 years! Sometimes an angel moved the water in the pool. The first sick person into the moving water would be healed.

Jesus spoke to the man who had been sick for 38 years. The man wanted to be well. But someone else always got into the moving water first. So, Jesus healed the sick man. The man picked up his mat and began to walk! Jesus can do amazing things!

JOHN 5:1-9

Anne McCourt, 10
Belfast, N. Ireland

Jesus Raises Lazarus from Death

Jesus' friend Lazarus was very sick. Jesus went to see him. But when Jesus got there, Lazarus had died. Lazarus' sisters, Mary and Martha, and their friends were all very sad and crying. Jesus asked them to take Him where Lazarus was buried. Jesus was very sad, too. He cried.

Then Jesus told the people to move the stone away from the door of the tomb. Jesus shouted, "Lazarus, come out!" Then Lazarus, who had been dead, walked out of the tomb. He was alive! Jesus is even more powerful than death.

JOHN 11:17-44

Gayle McGlynn, 6
Dublin, Ireland

The Last Supper

Jesus and His followers were eating the Passover Feast. Jesus said sadly, "One of you will turn against me." The followers did not know which one of them Jesus meant.

John asked, "Lord, who will turn against you?" Jesus dipped a piece of bread in a dish. He said He would give the bread to the one who would turn against him. Jesus gave the bread to Judas. Then Judas left.

Jesus told His followers, "Love each other as I have loved you. People will know you are my followers if you love each other."

JOHN 13:21-35

Janell L. Blea, 10
Denver, Colorado, USA

Peter Denies Jesus

Jesus and His followers were in a grove of olive trees. Judas knew where they were. So, he brought the soldiers there to arrest Jesus. The soldiers tied Jesus up and took Him to court.

Peter waited outside in the courtyard. Three times people asked Peter if he was one of Jesus' followers. But each time Peter said, "No, I'm not!" The third time Peter said he wasn't Jesus' follower, a rooster crowed. Jesus had told Peter that he would deny Him three times before the rooster crowed. When Peter heard the rooster, Jesus looked straight at him. And Peter was very ashamed of himself. He went away and cried. We should never say that we don't know Jesus.

JOHN 18:1-3, 12-13; LUKE 22:54-62

Carlos Alberto Garcia Forero, 11
Guatemala, Guatemala

Jesus Is Sent to Pilate

The Jews took Jesus to Pilate to be killed. Pilate questioned Him. But he could find no reason to kill Jesus. Pilate wanted to let Him go free. But the Jews wanted Jesus to die.

So, Pilate had his soldiers whip Jesus. The soldiers put a fake crown made of sharp thorns on His head. They put a purple robe on Him. They hit Jesus in the face. The soldiers said, "Hail! King of the Jews!" They hurt Jesus and laughed at Him.

Pilate tried again to free Jesus. But the Jewish leaders kept shouting, "Kill Him on a cross!" Finally, Pilate turned Jesus over to the Jews to be killed. This was all part of God's plan to save people.

JOHN 18:28-19:16

Jon Adams, 11
Lebanon, Indiana, USA

Jesus Dies

The soldiers took Jesus to a hill outside of Jerusalem called "The Place of the Skull." They made Jesus carry His own cross. The soldiers nailed Jesus to the cross. Two thieves were also hung on crosses, one on each side of Jesus.

Jesus' mother and some other women stood near the cross. Jesus' follower, John, was there, too. Jesus asked John to take care of His mother after He died. Jesus was sure everything had been done as the Scriptures said. He said, "It is finished." Then He bowed His head and died for us.

JOHN 19:16b-30

Marissa Young, 11
Anchorage, Alaska, USA

Jesus Is Buried

Later, a man named Joseph from Arimathea asked Pilate for Jesus' body. Joseph was a secret follower of Jesus. He kept it a secret because he was afraid of the Jews. Pilate gave him permission to take Jesus' body down from the cross.

Joseph and his friend Nicodemus took Jesus' body away. They wrapped Jesus' body with many spices in pieces of linen cloth. Then they put His body in a new tomb. It was in a garden near where Jesus died. But that's not how the story ends!

JOHN 19:38-42

Hazel Joy Esmilla, 12
Pasig, Metro Manila, Philippines

Jesus Lives Again!

Early on the first day of the week, Mary Magdalene went to Jesus' tomb. It was still dark outside. Mary saw that the large stone had been moved away from the tomb. So, she ran to tell Jesus' followers.

Peter and John ran to the tomb. They went inside. There they saw the linen cloths that had been around Jesus' body and head. Then the followers went back home. But Mary stood outside the tomb crying. She looked in the tomb and saw two angels. Then, when she turned around, she saw Jesus. He was alive! Jesus talked to Mary. Then she went to tell His followers that Jesus was alive again.

JOHN 20:1-18

Ben Ferguson, 8
Lincoln, Nebraska, USA

Jesus Appears to Thomas

After Jesus came back to life, He appeared to some of His followers. But Thomas was not with them. Jesus showed the followers the nail scars in His hands and the scar in His side. The men told Thomas, "We saw the Lord." But Thomas said he would not believe them until he saw and touched Jesus' scars himself.

About a week later, Jesus came to the followers again. This time Thomas was there. Jesus said to Thomas, "Put your finger here and touch my scars. Stop doubting and believe!" Then Thomas believed Jesus had been raised from death. "You believe because you can see me," Jesus said, "but people who believe without seeing me will be truly happy." We should never doubt Jesus either.

JOHN 20:24-29

Elissa Thomas, 9
Knoxville, Tennessee, USA

Jesus Goes Back to Heaven

The apostles were with Jesus. He said to them, "The Holy Spirit will come to you soon. You will receive power. You will be my witnesses here in Jerusalem. Then you'll go into the nearby areas. Finally, you will go into all of the world."

Then Jesus was lifted up into heaven. A cloud hid Him from their sight. They were staring into the sky where Jesus had gone. Suddenly, two men in white clothes stood beside them. "Why are you staring into the sky?" they asked. "Jesus will come back just as you saw Him go."

ACTS 1:6-11

Rebecca Fielding, 10
Milton Keynes, England

The Holy Spirit Comes

The day of Pentecost came. The followers were together. Suddenly a noise came from heaven. It sounded like a strong wind blowing. It was so loud that it filled up the whole house. Then they saw something that looked like flames of fire over each person there. The followers were filled with the Holy Spirit. He was helping them to speak different languages.

There were religious Jews staying in Jerusalem. They were from all over the world. When they heard the sound of wind, a crowd gathered. Then each person heard in his own language about the great things God had done. And they were all amazed!

ACTS 2:1-12

Laura Shively, 9
Shreveport, Louisiana, USA

Peter Heals a Crippled Beggar

Peter and John went to the Temple to pray. Nearby sat a man who had been crippled since birth. The crippled man was at the gate every day. He begged for money from people going to the Temple.

The man asked Peter and John for money. Peter said, "We don't have any money. But we have something else to give you. In the name of Jesus, stand up and walk!" The man's feet immediately grew strong. He jumped up and began walking! God helped Peter heal the crippled man. And all the people were surprised.

ACTS 3:1-16

Lisa Giuffre, 10
Norcross, Georgia, USA

Jesus' Followers Share

Jesus' followers shared everything they had with each other. Some people owned fields or houses. Those people sold their property. They brought the money they received to the church leaders, who were called apostles. The apostles made sure each person had everything he needed to live.

Joseph was one of the believers who sold his field and gave the money to the apostles. The apostles called him Barnabas, which means "one who encourages." Joseph's actions encouraged others to share. We should share with each other, too.

ACTS 4:32-37

Leylangela Goncalves, 10
San Antonio de los Altos, Venezuela

Apostles in Prison

The apostles did many miracles for the people. All the people were saying good things about them. Many men and women believed in the Lord.

A group of Jews called the Sadducees became very jealous of the apostles. They threw the apostles in jail. But during the night, an angel opened the doors of the jail. He led the apostles outside. Then he told them to go preach in the Temple.

The next morning the Sadducees went to the prison. But the apostles were not there! The Sadducees heard that the apostles were teaching in the Temple again. God's message is too powerful to be stopped!

ACTS 5:12-25

Robyn Mogan, 9
Vancouver, British Columbia, Canada

A Nobleman Is Saved

An angel told Philip to go to the road that goes from Jerusalem to Gaza. There Philip saw a nobleman from Ethiopia riding in a chariot. The nobleman had been to Jerusalem to worship. Now he was going home. He was reading the Scriptures.

Philip asked the man, "Do you understand what you're reading?" The nobleman said, "I need someone to explain it to me." So, Philip told him all about Jesus. When they came to some water, the nobleman asked Philip to baptize him. Then he went happily on his way home. Obeying God makes you happy.

ACTS 8:26-40

Tepnimit Pimpang, 13
Bangkok, Thailand

Saul Meets Jesus

Saul went around Jerusalem trying to frighten Jesus' followers. He told the followers he would kill them! Then he decided to go to Damascus to hurt Jesus' followers there. On his way to Damascus, a bright light from heaven suddenly flashed around him. Saul fell to the ground. He couldn't see! Then Saul heard a voice say, "Why are you trying to hurt me?" Saul said, "Who are you, Lord?"

The voice answered, "I am Jesus. I am the One you are trying to hurt. Get up now and go to Damascus." Saul waited in Damascus for three days. Then God sent Ananias to him. Ananias put his hands on Saul, and Saul could see again. Then he was baptized and followed Jesus.

ACTS 9:1-19

Siritip Harntaweewongsa, 9
Bangkok, Thailand

Tabitha Lives Again!

Once there was a follower of
Jesus named Tabitha. She helped the
poor people and others by sewing for
them. Tabitha got sick and died. Her
friends sent for Peter to come.

When Peter arrived, they took him
upstairs. Peter sent everyone out of
the room. He kneeled and prayed.
Then he said, "Tabitha, stand up!" She
opened her eyes, and Peter helped her
stand up. Then Peter called Tabitha's
friends. They saw that Tabitha was
alive again! People everywhere heard
about Tabitha and believed in the
Lord.

ACTS 9:36-43

Angela Barry, 15
Belfast, N. Ireland

Peter Has a Vision

Just before lunch, Peter went up on the roof to pray. He was hungry and wanted to eat. But while the food was being prepared, Peter had a vision. He saw heaven open up and something coming down. It looked like a big sheet being lowered by its four corners. In the sheet were all kinds of animals, reptiles and birds. A voice said, "Get up, Peter; kill and eat." But Peter said, "No, Lord! I have never eaten unholy or unclean food."

The voice said, "God has made these things clean. Don't call them unholy." This happened three times. Then Peter understood that God loves all people everywhere. We should, too.

ACTS 10:9-16

Allison Daigle, 10½
Amherst, New Hampshire, USA

Paul and Silas

Paul and Silas had been put in prison because they were teaching about Jesus. The jailer put them far inside the jail. He pinned their feet down between large blocks of wood.

About midnight Paul and Silas were praying and singing songs to God. Suddenly, there was an earthquake! It shook the jail. All the prisoners' chains fell off. The jailer woke up and thought the prisoners had escaped. He started to kill himself. But Paul shouted, "Don't hurt yourself! We're all here." That night, the jailer and everyone in his house were saved.

ACTS 16:20-34

Michael Mohsen, 8
Paris, France

Paul Escapes

A group of 40 Jewish men pledged not to eat or drink until they had killed Paul. Paul's nephew heard about the plan. He told the commander of the Roman army guarding Paul. The commander ordered his army to take Paul safely to the governor. They took 200 soldiers, 70 horsemen and 200 men with spears to protect Paul. And they left at nine o'clock at night.

The soldiers took Paul to another city that night. The next day the horsemen took Paul to the governor. God had helped Paul escape!

ACTS 23:12-33

Ana Elizabeth Martinez, 10
Reynosa Tamps, Mexico

Paul's Shipwreck

Paul was being taken to Rome for a trial. He and the soldier guarding him traveled on a big ship. A terrible storm hit, and they had to throw everything overboard. At last the storm was too great, and they had to let the wind blow them around.

On the fourteenth night, they came close to land. They dropped anchor until morning. At dawn they tried to sail the ship onto the beach. But the ship hit a sandbar. Huge waves broke the ship apart. Everyone jumped in the water and swam safely to shore. God had taken care of them all.

ACTS 27:1-2, 13-15, 27-44

Steven Giron, 12
Cascais, Portugal

Christians Should Obey Laws

All of you must obey the laws of the land. Obey government rulers because God has given them the power to rule. If you do things against the government, you are really doing them against God. People who do right things are not afraid of rulers. The rulers are God's servants to help you. But if you do wrong things, then be afraid. The rulers will punish you.

Also, pay your taxes. Rulers are working for God. Show respect and honor to them all. That way, you show respect and honor to God.

ROMANS 13:1-7

Lee Gessner, IV, 13
Grand Rapids, Michigan, USA

Love Others

Love is the best way of all. You might be able to speak in different languages. You might be able to tell the future. You might even be really smart. But if you don't show love to others, these things don't matter at all.

A person who loves is patient and kind. He isn't jealous and doesn't brag. A person who loves is not rude or selfish. He does not become angry easily or remember when someone is mean to him. Love is not happy with bad, but is happy with good.

Three things will never end: faith, hope and love. But love is the greatest thing of all.

1 CORINTHIANS 13:1-13

Michael Hager, 9
Louisville, Kentucky, USA

Obey Your Parents

Children, you should obey your parents. The Lord wants you to. It is the right thing to do.

God's Word says this: "Honor your father and mother." This was the very first command that God gave with a promise. And here's the promise: "If you obey your parents, everything will be well with you. And you will have a long life on earth."

What a great and wonderful promise!

EPHESIANS 6:1-3

Sarah Thomas, 8
Williamsport, Pennsylvania, USA

The Armor of God

Be strong in the Lord! Wear God's armor. It helps you fight against the evil powers in the world. These evil powers are very strong. That's why you need God's armor to protect you. That way, when the fight is over, you will still be safe.

Telling the truth is like a belt that protects your waist. Living right protects you like a chest covering. The Good News about Jesus protects you like strong boots on your feet. And faith protects you like a shield against the devil's burning arrows. God's salvation protects your head like a helmet. And God's Word is like a sword to help you beat the devil.

EPHESIANS 6:10-18

Sarah Cobb, 11
Carrollton, Texas, USA

Be Happy

Always be happy in the Lord. Be gentle and kind. Don't worry about anything. Pray and ask God for everything you need. And when you pray, always give thanks. Then God will give you peace.

Think about good things. Think about what is true, honorable, right, pure, beautiful and respected. God will be with you if you do. Learn to be happy, no matter what. Be happy whether you are rich or poor. Be happy when you are full or hungry. Here's the secret: You can do any of these things through the strength of Christ Jesus!

PHILIPPIANS 4:4-13

Abigail Carneiro, 8
Nairobi, Kenya

Go To Church Meetings

We are all in God's family, called the church. We should think about each other. We should encourage each other and show love. We should help each other and do good things for other people.

Some people don't go to the meetings at the church. That is not good. You should go to the meetings at church so you can encourage each other. God is pleased when His people help and encourage each other.

HEBREWS 10:24-25

Jenny Monroe, 10
Decatur, Alabama, USA

Help Others

Keep on loving each other. You are brothers in Christ's family. Welcome strangers into your homes. Some people have done this and have welcomed angels without knowing it.

Don't forget about the people who are in prison. Care for them as if you were in prison yourself. And care for those who are suffering as if you were suffering with them.

Remember your leaders. They taught you God's message. Remember how they lived and died. Copy their faith in God. And always remember this: Jesus Christ is always the same— yesterday, today and forever. You can depend on Him.

HEBREWS 13:1-8

Ashley Lassiter, 10
Knoxville, Tennessee, USA

Be Careful What You Say

Sometimes we all say bad things. If a person never said anything wrong, he would be perfect. He would be able to control his whole body.

We put bits in horses' mouths to make them obey us. With a small bit we control the entire horse. Also, a very little rudder controls a huge ship. The tongue is like that. It's very small, but it brags about great things.

People can tame every kind of animal, bird, reptile and fish. But no one can tame the tongue. Praises to God and curses for others should not come from the same mouth. Be careful what you say!

JAMES 3:2-12

Renee Barham, 11
Jacksonville, Florida, USA

Do What's Right

All of you should live together in peace. Try to understand each other. Love each other as brothers do. Be kind and humble. Don't be mean to a person to pay him back for being mean to you. And do not insult someone to pay him back for insulting you. Instead, ask God to bless that person.

Always be ready to tell about Jesus to anyone who asks. Answer them in a gentle way with respect. Do things that are right. Then, anyone who says bad things about your good life in Christ will be ashamed of what they said. It is better to suffer for doing good than wrong. Do what's right!

1 PETER 3:8-17

Alec Tefertiller, 12
Ft. Worth, Texas, USA

Choose to Do Good

Peter 3:8-17

God Is Love

Dear friends, we should love each other. That's because love comes from God. The person who loves has become God's child and knows God. Whoever does not love, does not know God.

This is how God showed His love for us: He sent His only Son, Jesus, to take away our sins. That is how much God loved us! So, now we must also love each other. It's true that no one has ever seen God. But if we love each other, it will be like God living in us. And God's love is made perfect in us. Love others!

1 JOHN 4:7-12

Kirstie Jay, 9
Altoona, Pennsylvania, USA

Jesus Is Coming Again!

God's angel told John, "Listen! I am coming soon! I will bring rewards with me. I will repay each person for what he has done. I am the beginning of all things. And I am the end of all things. People who have obeyed me will be blessed. They will get to eat the fruit from the tree of life. They can go through the gates into the heavenly city. But those who do evil will be left outside the city.

"I, Jesus, have sent my angel to tell you these things. I am the bright, morning star. Yes, I am coming soon." Come, Lord Jesus!

REVELATION 22:10-21

Elizabeth Preece, 10½
Milton Keynes, England

Contributing Artists

God Made Our World
Courtney Cooper, 7
Fort Worth, Texas, USA
Adam and Eve
Tiffany Babich, 11
Los Alamos, New Mexico, USA
Garden of Eden
Ana Valadares, 13
Washington, DC, USA
Man's Big Mistake
Shelley Croft, 10
Tigard, Oregon, USA
The First Brothers
Amy Beckman, 10½
Boise, Idaho, USA
Noah's Boat
Hanan Jamalieh, 9
Nazareth, Israel
The Flood
Basil Khalil, 9
Nazareth, Israel
The Flood Ends
Dan Goodwin, 9
Upper Darby, Pennsylvania, USA
Tower of Babel
Craig Oertel, 11
Atlanta, Georgia, USA
Abram and Lot
Lilian Wangai, 8
Nairobi, Kenya
Esau Sells His Rights
Elsa Buckley, 9
Seattle, Washington, USA
Jacob's Dream
Grant Gardner, 11
Konigstein, W. Germany
Joseph's Special Coat
Abbie Ballou, 8
Springfield, Missouri, USA
Joseph is Sold
Emily Francis Jones, 9
Trinity, Alabama, USA

Joseph Explains the King's Dream
Megan Culler, 10
Dublin, Ohio, USA
Joseph Rules Egypt
Joseph Griffith, 10
Columbus, Ohio, USA
Baby Moses
Paul Edgerton, 9
Roseville, Minnesota, USA
A Burning Bush
Alexander Martinez, 8
Brooklyn, New York, USA
Ten Terrible Plagues
Samantha Bohannon, 10
Decatur, Alabama, USA
Leaving Egypt
Susan Turner, 8½
Winnipeg, Manitoba, Canada
God Sends Manna
Vera Marosi, 8
Nairobi, Kenya
Water from a Rock
Aron Mueller, 7
Anchorage, Alaska, USA
God's Ten Laws
Travis Ashley, 9
Decatur, Alabama, USA
The Gold Calf
Kacy Etheridge, 11
Oak Ridge, Tennessee, USA
The Twelve Spies
Jennifer Holland, 7
N. Little Rock, Arkansas, USA
A Talking Donkey
Micah Beard, 9
Bangor, N. Ireland
Rahab Helps the Spies
David Richardson, 12
Washington, England
The Sun Stands Still
Ashley Miner, 6
Terre Haute, Indiana, USA

Gideon's Brave 300
Raymond Kotzatoski, 8
Altoona, Pennsylvania, USA
Samson and Delilah
Penny Broadhurst, 9
Hampsthwaite, England
The Story of Ruth
Minda Johnson, 8
St. Paul, Minnesota, USA
David and Goliath
Jamie Harrison, 12
Omaha, Nebraska, USA
David and Jonathan
David Shaffer, 12
Cotuit, Massachusetts, USA
King Solomon's Wisdom
Katie A. Perkins, 8
Ft. Worth, Texas, USA
Elijah Stops the Rain
Kelly Taylor, 8
Springfield, Missouri, USA
Elijah and the Prophets of Baal
Kristin Mueller, 11
Anchorage, Alaska, USA
A Boy Lives Again
Patrick Williams, 8
Shreveport, Louisiana, USA
Queen Esther Saves Her People
Josse Rocio Santizo Gil, 10
Guatemala, Guatemala
Job is Faithful
Cory Sheldon, 12
Stow, Ohio, USA
My Shepherd
Sarah Ratliff, 7
Alamogordo, New Mexico, USA
Advice to Children
Jennifer Yactor, 11
Los Alamos, New Mexico, USA
The Blazing Furnace
Jeremy Young, 11
Oklahoma City, Oklahoma, USA
Writing on the Wall
Steven Thomas, 11
Ft. Worth, Texas, USA
Daniel in the Lion's Den
Yuriko Emaru, 8
Iruma Shi, Japan

Jonah and the Big Fish
Sarah Carr, 7
Asuncion, Paraguay
An Angel Visits Mary
Sarah Gentry, 11
Somerset, New Jersey, USA
Jesus is Born
Ryan Gates, 11
Cuyahoga Falls, Ohio, USA
Shepherds Hear About Jesus
Lisa Paden, 11
Libby, Montana, USA
Wise Men Come to Jesus
Tomoko Yamaguchi, 8
Tokorozawa, Japan
Escape to Egypt
Laura Clark, 9
Woodville, Ohio, USA
The Boy Jesus
Jon-Marc Harrison, 10
Omaha, Nebraska, USA
John the Baptist
Andrew Beckwith, 7
Higashi Kurume, Japan
Jesus is Baptized
Valerie Valenzuela, 9
Nairobi, Kenya
Jesus is Tempted
Meggie Anderton, 8
Knoxville, Tennessee, USA
The Lord's Prayer
Kareen Hansen, 9
Nairobi, Kenya
Jesus' Sermon on the Mountain
Saida Helaine Cedeno Freites, 10
San Antonio de los Altos, Venezuela
Jesus Feeds More Than 5,000 People
Merry Adis Prasetya Polly, 11
Kupang, NTT, Indonesia
Jesus Walks on Water
Shannon Payne, 9
Taos, New Mexico, USA
Jesus Enters Jerusalem
Pamela E. Villegas, 10
Pasig, Metro Manila, Philippines
Jesus Cleans out the Temple
Christen Williams, 11
Burleson, Texas, USA

Paul Escapes
Ana Elizabeth Martinez, 10
Reynosa Tamps, Mexico
Paul's Shipwreck
Steven Giron, 12
Cascais, Portugal
Christians Should Obey Laws
Lee Gessner, IV, 13
Grand Rapids, Michigan, USA
Love Others
Michael Hager, 9
Louisville, Kentucky, USA
Obey Your Parents
Sarah Thomas, 8
Williamsport, Pennsylvania, USA
The Armor of God
Sarah Cobb, 11
Carrollton, Texas, USA
Be Happy
Abigail Carneiro, 8
Nairobi, Kenya
Go To Church Meetings
Jenny Monroe, 10
Decatur, Alabama, USA
Help Others
Ashley Lassiter, 10
Knoxville, Tennessee, USA
Be Careful What You Say
Renee Barham, 11
Jacksonville, Florida, USA
Do What's Right
Alec Tefertiller, 12
Ft. Worth, Texas, USA
God is Love
Kirstie Jay, 9
Altoona, Pennsylvania, USA
Jesus is Coming Again!
Elizabeth Preece, 10½
Milton Keynes, England

God likes for us to learn stories about Him. Do you like the story of *David and Goliath*? What about *Jesus Walking on Water*? You can draw your favorite Bible stories on the following pages. Or, you can draw pictures about things God has done for you. This is a special Bible so you can color in it. Remember to write the name of each story at the top of the page. At the bottom of the page, write your name and age.

God bless you!